THIS BOOK BELONGS TO

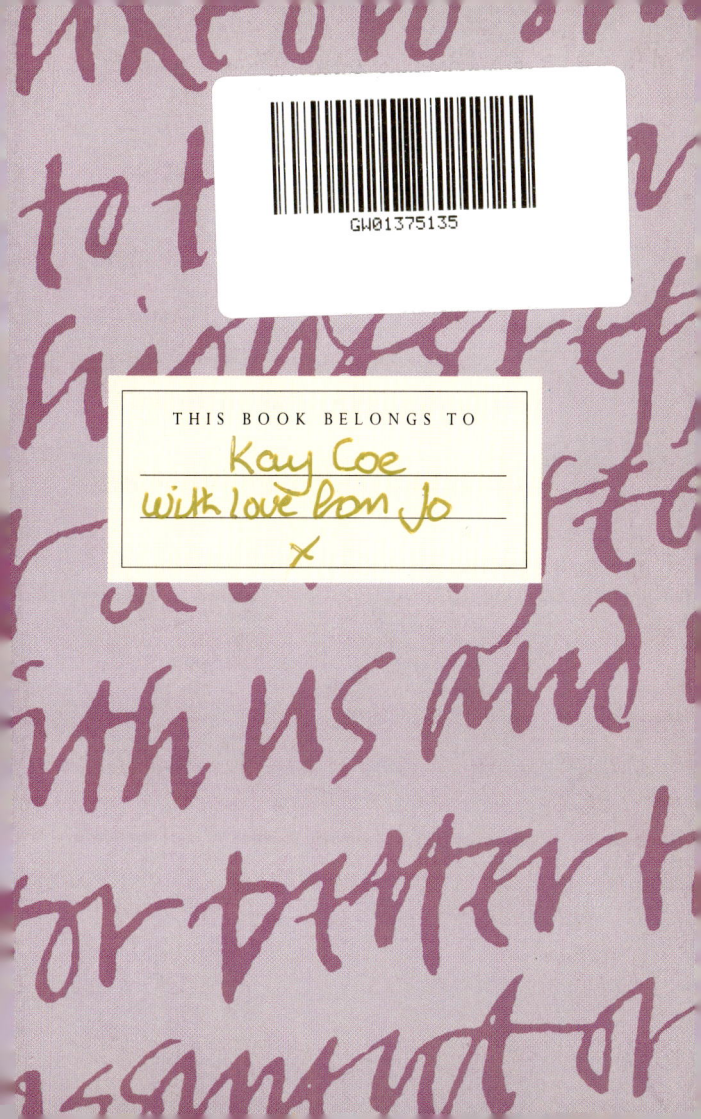

Kay Coe
with love from Jo
x

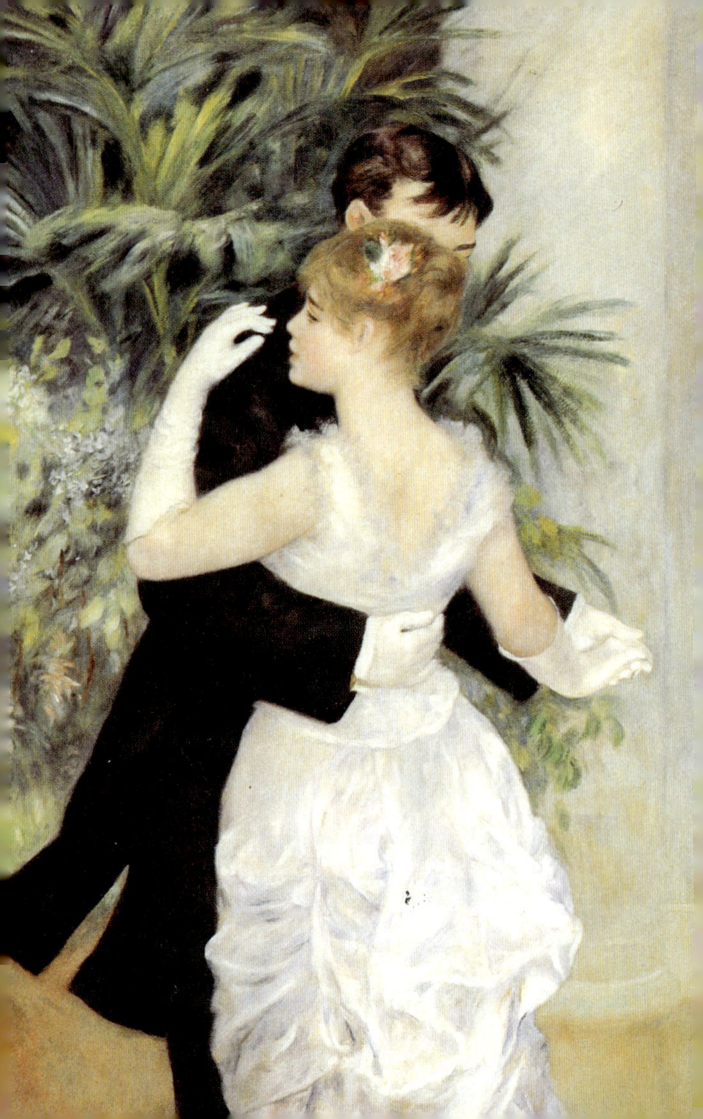

In Praise of
FRIENDS

JARROLD
PUBLISHING

Old Friends are like old shoes,
    They are so fitted to the years
They know our highest efforts
    And discern our secret fears.
They've walked with us and waited
    When we aimed for better things,
Through embarrassment or glory,
    Poor as paupers, proud as kings.
And though for various reasons
    Shoes wear out and friendships end
We lose part of our lives
    Each time we quarrel with a friend.

FRIENDSHIP

Kathleen Partridge

You can't buy friendship,
It's worth more than gold,
And its value increases
As true friends grow old.

Phyllis Ellison

IN PRAISE OF FRIENDS

FISHING

Arthur Hunter

IN PRAISE OF FRIENDS

AT THE THEATRE
James Hayllar 1829–1920

IN PRAISE OF FRIENDS

You make more friends by becoming interested in other people than by trying to interest other people in yourself.

Dale Carnegie

It is a good thing to be rich and a good thing to be strong but it is a better thing to be loved of many friends.

Links of gold may dull and sever
but links of friendship
last for ever.

LE DÉJEUNER
SUR L'HERBE
Claude Monet 1840–1926

Treat your friends
as you do your picture,
and place them in their best light.

Jennie Jerome Churchill

One whose thoughts are a little cleaner,
One whose mind is a little keener,
One who avoids those things that are meaner,
That's what I call a friend.

So long as we love, we serve.
So long as we are loved by others, we are indispensable;
and no man is useless while he has a friend.

Robert Louis Stevenson

IN PRAISE OF FRIENDS

DANSE À LA CAMPAGNE
Pierre-Auguste Renoir 1841–1919

If only all the world could learn
    The simple art of living;
They'd know that each was born to fill
    His daily life in giving.
For only those who love to give
    Have ever really learned to live.

It is better to have one friend of great value
than many friends who are good for nothing.

It's nice to have a laugh together sometimes,
    but to be real friends,
    folk have to weep together.

When our friends are present,
we ought to treat them well:
and when they are absent,
to speak of them well.

Epictetus

To have a good friend is the purest of all God's gifts, for it is a love that has no exchange of payment.

Frances Farmer

A true friend is the greatest of all blessings, and the one which we take least thought to acquire.

Duc de la Rochefoucauld

A friend is never known until needed.
God evidently does not intend us all
to be rich or powerful or great,
but he does intend us all to be friends.

Ralph Waldo Emerson

AT THE WELL
Egisto Ferroni 1835–1912

THE BALL ON SHIPBOARD
James Tissot 1836–1902

IN PRAISE OF FRIENDS

Of all the things which wisdom
provides to make life entirely happy,
much the greatest is the possession
of friendship.

Epicurus

True happiness consists
not in the multitude of friends
but in the worth and choice.

Ben Jonson

IN PRAISE OF FRIENDS

TWO LADIES
Rosa Brett fl.1858–1881

A real friend is the one who walks in when the rest of the world walks out.

Walter Windrell

A problem shared is a problem halved.
A joy that is shared is a joy that is doubled.

When you meet a man, you judge him by his clothes;
When you leave, you judge him by his heart.

Russian proverb

Silence makes the real conversations between friends. Not the saying, but the never needing to say, is what counts.

M.L. Runbeck

In prosperity our friends know us;
In adversity we know our friends.

J.M. Barrie

IN PRAISE OF FRIENDS

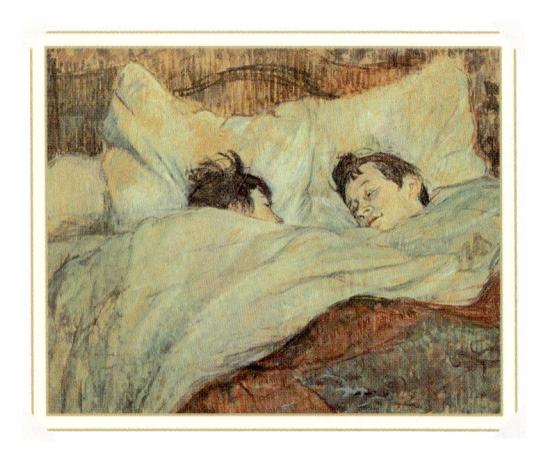

LE LIT

Henri de Toulouse-Lautrec 1864–1901

If a man does not make new acquaintances
as he advances through life,
he will soon find himself alone.
A man, Sir, should keep his friendships
in constant repair.

Samuel Johnson

IN PRAISE OF FRIENDS

PICNIC IN MAY

Szinyei Merse Pal

$\mathcal{H}$ast thou a friend? Visit him often, for thorns and brushwood obstruct the road which no one treads.

Old Eastern proverb

Greater love hath no man than this,
that a man lay down his life for his friends.

John 15:13

Try to do to others as you would have them do to you, and do not be discouraged if they fail sometimes.

Charles Dickens

Real friends are those who,
when you've made
a fool of yourself,
don't feel you've done
a permanent job.

A friend is a person with whom I may be sincere; before him, I may think aloud.

Ralph Waldo Emerson

IN PRAISE OF FRIENDS

YOUR MOVE!

Giovanni Garinei b.1846

If you judge people, you have no time to love them.

Mother Teresa

IN PRAISE OF FRIENDS

LA BARQUE

Claude Monet 1840–1926

*T*rouble is a sieve through which
we sift our acquaintances.
Those too big to pass through are our friends.

Arlene Francis

Friendship is the gift of the gods,
and the most precious boon to man.

Benjamin Disraeli

Who seeks
a faultless friend
remains friendless.

Turkish proverb

IN PRAISE OF FRIENDS

ADMIRING THE LOCKET

Pio Ricci 1850–1919

Friendship is honey – but don't eat it all.

Moroccan proverb

What is a friend?
– A single soul dwelling in two bodies.

Aristotle

People are lonely
because they build walls
instead of bridges.

J.F. Newton

Fate chooses your relations,
you choose your friends.

A SOCIABLE
AFTERNOON ON THE BEACH
Frederik H. Kaemmerer 1839–1902

If you have one true friend,
you have more than your fair share.

Thomas Fuller

ALSO IN THIS SERIES

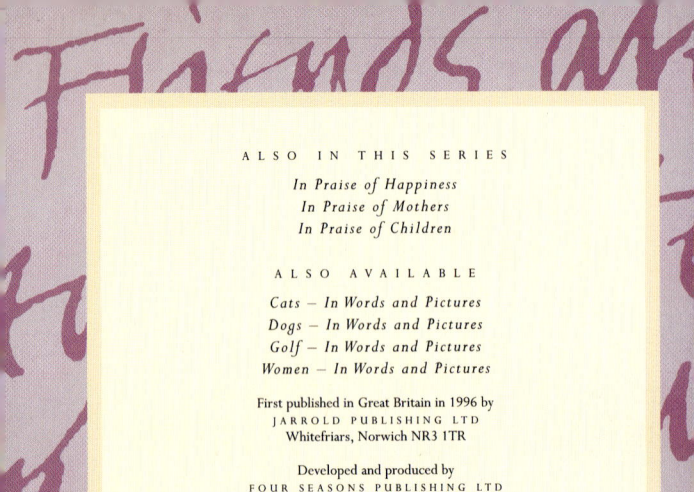

In Praise of Happiness
In Praise of Mothers
In Praise of Children

ALSO AVAILABLE

Cats – In Words and Pictures
Dogs – In Words and Pictures
Golf – In Words and Pictures
Women – In Words and Pictures

First published in Great Britain in 1996 by
JARROLD PUBLISHING LTD
Whitefriars, Norwich NR3 1TR

Developed and produced by
FOUR SEASONS PUBLISHING LTD
1 Durrington Avenue, London SW20 8NT

Text research by *Pauline Barrett*
Designed in association with *The Bridgewater Book Company*
Edited by *David Notley* and *Peter Bridgewater*
Picture research by *Vanessa Fletcher*
Printed in Dubai

Copyright © 1996 Four Seasons Publishing Ltd

All rights reserved.

ISBN 0-7117-0864-9

ACKNOWLEDGEMENTS

Four Seasons Publishing Ltd would like to thank all those
who kindly gave permission to reproduce the words and visual
material in this book; copyright holders have been identified
where possible and we apologise for any inadvertent omissions.

We would particularly like to thank the following
for the use of pictures: *e.t. archive*, *Fine Art Photographic Library*.

Front Cover: THE FLORISTS, *Stephano Novo* 19th century
Title Page and Back Cover: TOWN AND COUNTRY, *George Henry Boughton* 1833–1905
Frontispiece: DANSE À LA VILLE, *Pierre-Auguste Renoir* 1841–1919